Titles in the series:

DELETE
TIM COLLINS

IN THE STARS
ECHO FREER

KEEPER
ANN EVANS

KILL ORDER
DANIEL BLYTHE

LAST YEAR
IAIN McLAUGHLIN

PARADISE
TIM COLLINS

S/HE
CATHERINE BRUTON

THE CRAVING
CLIFF McNISH

Badger Publishing Limited, Oldmedow Road, Hardwick Industrial Estate, King's Lynn PE30 4JJ

Telephone: 01438 791037

www.badgerlearning.co.uk

DELETE

TIM COLLINS

Delete ISBN 978-1-78464-704-9

Publisher: Susan Ross
Senior Editor: Danny Pearson
Copyediting: Cambridge Publishing Management Ltd
Designer: Bigtop Design Ltd
Cover: Image Source / Alamy

2 4 6 8 10 9 7 5 3 1

CHAPTER 1
THE STRANGER

The boy approached me on the corner of Station Road and North Street.

'Ryan,' he said, 'we need to talk.'

This was awkward. He seemed to know me, but I had no idea who he was. I did my best to smile.

'Why haven't you called?' he asked.

This was really awkward. He really seemed to know me.

'Er… I'm struggling a bit here,' I said.

He was tall with short blond hair and green eyes. I would have found him sort of cute if he hadn't been so weird.

'Yeah,' he said, 'I'm struggling too. I've been struggling for the last two weeks.'

I had no idea what to say. Maybe he was disturbed and wanted my help. I'd feel bad if I walked away, but I had no idea what else to do.

'I need to go,' I said, 'but I hope you can find someone to help you soon.'

The boy grabbed my arm. I pulled back, but his grip was too strong. 'Stop playing games,' he said. 'You know what I'm trying to say.'

I managed to yank my arm free.

'I think we should get back together,' said the boy. He was blinking tears from his eyes. 'Happy now?'

I rushed away down the street. I'd been meaning to go to the shops, but the strange boy had freaked me out so much that I just wanted to get home.

Every time I glanced over my shoulder I saw him standing there and staring.

What was all that stuff about us getting back together? It was like I was his ex-boyfriend and he was trying to get me back. But I'd never had a boyfriend. I'd never even told anyone I was gay, except Mum and Dad. And that didn't exactly go brilliantly.

I spent the rest of the day lying in bed and wondering about the boy. Was that his way of meeting new guys? It was a really weird one.

The most likely explanation was that I really looked like his ex. I wondered if I'd ever run into this mysterious double of mine.

I was still thinking about the stranger when a text came through:

Adam here. So why did you act like that today?

I didn't know anyone with that name, so I guessed it was a wrong number. It must have been my day to be mistaken for random strangers.

But then I got another one:

I meant what I said about us getting back together... Adam.

Now I was worried. This was the same guy. He knew my number. What else did he know about me?

I'd heard about stalkers. They're convinced they know you and they turn violent if you say otherwise.

The obvious thing to do next was go to the police, but what had this Adam guy actually done? He hadn't attacked me, or even threatened me.

On the other hand, I wouldn't feel safe as long as he was sending these crazy texts.

I sent a message back:

Stop hassling me. I don't know who you are but I'll go to the police.

He got back to me right away:

I know things didn't end well between us, but that's insane.

I was insane? He was the one who'd approached a stranger in the street and told him he wanted to get back together.

I didn't want to engage with this Adam guy. I told myself it would be safer to just shut down the conversation.

I sent him a final text:

Don't contact me again.

It didn't work. He kept sending messages, all based around his fantasy that we were once an item.

When I ignored them, he started calling. Over and over again. My battery died and by the time I'd found my charger I had 12 missed calls.

I wondered if I should tell Mum and Dad, but I hate talking to them about personal stuff. The night I came out to them they were both so quiet that I had to mute the TV and tell them again because I thought they hadn't heard. Dad told me I was still too young to worry about any of that stuff, then he grabbed the remote and turned the sound back up.

Never mind congratulating me or telling me it was all fine, they just went straight back to their quiz show and kept on muttering the answers under their breath.

I was about to take one of Adam's calls and tell him again to stop hassling me when he changed tactic. He sent a photo instead.

I stared at it in disbelief.

It was a picture of us together. We were in my bedroom, perched on the edge of my bed.

Adam had his right arm stretched out to take the picture and he was grinning into the lens. I was next to him, smiling too, with my arm around his shoulders.

It wasn't fake. It was a real photo, taken in the very room I was sitting in. And yet I had no memory of it at all.

CHAPTER 2
THE CLINIC

The only explanation was that I had a memory problem. This kind of thing could happen to me all the time for all I knew.

I rooted around in my desk drawers, looking for evidence of my condition. Some letter from a doctor or instructions I'd written to myself. But there was nothing like that. In fact, I could remember every little detail about everything I saw.

There was a batch of stickers from the World Cup before last. I remembered swapping spares in class, and completing every country except

Uruguay, Greece and South Korea. There was a birthday card from my great aunt Debbie with an Amazon gift card I'd never used. There was the key to a bike lock I'd got rid of years ago. I'd thrown the lock away but couldn't bring myself to get rid of the key.

So much for my theory about memory problems. I could recall every tiny detail about my life except who Adam was and why we were in a picture together.

There was a scrap of paper in my top drawer with 'Sat 2.30 LC' scrawled on it in my handwriting. I wondered if it had something to do with Adam. But no matter how much I thought about it, I couldn't remember anything about the message.

I was scared to go out the next day, but I needed to do something. I was going crazy sitting in my room and thinking about it all.

I walked through the park, down North Street, and turned right into Station Road. I was nervous about Adam appearing again, but there was no sign of him.

I kept going and going, figuring that I might stop worrying if I exhausted myself.

I walked down a long straight road that ran alongside some train tracks until I reached an industrial park on the east of town. I'd never been there before, but I found myself striding down a road called Olympic Avenue, which took me past blocky buildings with names like 'Williams Solutions' and 'Taylor Information Limited'. I had no idea what companies like that did, but they sounded boring.

I promised myself I wouldn't end up in one of those places, counting down the years until retirement. I don't know exactly what I want to do, except that I want to get out of this town, and I don't want to work in 'solutions' or 'information', whatever they are.

While I was thinking all this, I found I'd come to a stop in front of a wide white building. A high wire fence stretched around it. The only gap was manned by a security guard who was staring at me with his arms folded.

According to a small plaque attached to the fence, the building was called 'The Loftus Clinic'. I wondered why I'd felt drawn here. It was as though my feet had guided me.

I wandered up to the security guard, wondering if I could get him to give anything away. Before I could say anything he asked for something called my 'Unique Reference Number'. When I said I didn't have one, he looked away and refused to speak further.

I gave up and went back home. It was only when I was passing through the town centre again that I made the connection. The note I'd scrawled had read 'Sat 2.30 LC'. The 'LC' bit could mean The Loftus Clinic. So maybe I *had* been there before, one Saturday afternoon. And maybe some part of my brain remembered it and had led me there.

It wasn't getting any clearer, but I had a feeling the answers were inside that huge white building. I needed to find a way to get inside The Loftus Clinic.

CHAPTER 3

THE NUMBER

Back in my room, I searched online for information about The Loftus Clinic. There wasn't much. They had a website, but you needed a reference number to get into it.

Without one, all you could see was a picture of the building itself and some cheesy stock shots of happy families and smiling old people.

They didn't even list their services. Weren't websites meant to advertise products?

I looked for mentions of the place on other sites, but there were loads of doctors and dentists with the same name and it was impossible to sift through them all.

I wondered if Adam could tell me more. But if I did text him, he might take it as encouragement. I'd promised myself I wouldn't engage with him.

In the end my curiosity got the better of me. I sent him a quick message:

Ever heard of The Loftus Clinic?

He got back to me straight away:

Yeah, you mentioned it.

Then, a couple of minutes later:

Fine. You win.

And that was it. No further texts, no attempts to call.

The day before, Adam couldn't stop calling. Now I'd reached out to him, all I got were short texts that made no sense.

My brain was hurting from thinking about it. I tried to nap, but I couldn't drop off. Then I tried getting on with my history homework, but I couldn't focus.

I went back to searching around my room. There must have been something in there that I hadn't spotted.

I took all my clothes out of my wardrobe and went through the pockets, in case there was a receipt from the clinic stuffed into one.

I leafed through all my school books and box files, in case I'd written something in them.

Finally, I tried my bin. It was pretty grim. I fished out the smoothie bottles and crisp packets, and examined the crumpled bits of paper at the bottom.

A maths worksheet, a page from an essay, that the printer had chewed up, a bus timetable.

Underneath all these were some scraps of paper that had been torn into tiny pieces.

I lifted them out of the bin and pieced them back together on my carpet. It was like a jigsaw that smelled of stale fruit smoothies.

There were letters and numbers written on the tiny bits of paper in my handwriting. When I'd finally fitted them all together, they read:

Unique Reference Number 1784646172

That was what the guard had asked for! It would get me in, though I had no idea what I'd do after that.

I looked at my watch. It was unlikely that the clinic would be open after seven on a Sunday night. I'd have to leave it until after school the next day.

Time went really slowly that Monday. I couldn't focus on any of my lessons. I sat with Amy and Laura at lunch as usual, but I didn't say much. I wanted to tell them about everything that had happened, but I didn't know where to start.

What did I get up to this weekend? I met a crazy stalker who said he was my ex-boyfriend, but I can't go to the police because I think he might be right and it's all to do with a mysterious white building on the edge of town.

I listened to them compare notes about the hideous family parties they'd been dragged along to. I longed for a problem as simple as being embarrassed by a drunk aunt.

As soon as school was over I raced to the industrial estate and made my way to The Loftus Clinic.

The car parks of all the offices on Olympic Avenue were full. Smartly dressed men and woman were milling around the entrances, gazing at their phones.

The same security guard as before was on duty. I told him my reference number and he prodded a tablet. He nodded and pointed at the white building without saying anything.

I walked down a straight path of clean grey paving stones that was surrounded on both sides by neat grass. At the end, the wide automatic doors of the clinic swished aside.

I was in a gleaming white reception area with a curved plastic desk to my right and a bright corridor ahead.

I had no idea what I was doing. All I could think to do was approach the woman sitting behind the desk and tell her my reference number. I really hoped she wouldn't ask for any details about my visit.

The woman typed the number into her computer and told me someone would be with me in a minute. She pointed to a white leather sofa opposite her desk, and I strolled over and perched on the end.

Someone was about to come and see me and I had to work out what I was going to say. I considered trying to bluff my way through the meeting, but I decided it would be better to just tell the truth.

A woman in a white lab coat was ushering a middle-aged man along the corridor and out through the automatic doors. He looked confused and tired, like he'd just woken up after a long sleep.

Another woman in a white coat emerged. She had thick-rimmed glasses and long red hair that was tied back.

She looked at me. 'Ryan Watson?'

I nodded and followed her into an office on the left side of the corridor.

She took a seat behind a square white desk and I sat opposite. The woman tapped on her mouse and glanced at the desktop computer in front of her.

'I understand you're a patient of ours,' she said.

'I'm glad you understand,' I said, 'because I've got no idea what's going on. I found my reference number in my bin. I can't remember coming here before, but I must have done.'

The woman leaned back in her chair and rested her chin on her fingers. 'My advice would be to turn around and go home,' she said. 'Our services can be expensive. Any information I give you now could undo the valuable work we've done.'

I looked down at my feet to make her think I was considering it. The truth was I was no more likely to leave without finding out everything I could than I was to fly home.

'I need to know more,' I said. 'My mind won't be at rest until I find out what happened to me here.'

The woman nodded.

'I understand,' she said. 'The truth is that we offer a memory wipe service at this clinic. We take out a part of someone's life that's causing them pain. For example, if someone is having trouble coping with grief, we could erase the memory of the dead person.'

She turned back to her screen and tapped on her keyboard. 'OK, I'm looking through your case now and I can confirm that the person who arranged your treatment wanted the details to remain confidential.'

'Which person?' I asked.

'That would be one of the confidential details, I'm afraid,' said the woman.

'There must be something you can tell me,' I said.

'I don't know the ins and outs of every case we take on,' she said. 'We have over 100 members of staff and we take on dozens of new customers every day.'

She clicked her mouse a couple of times and said, 'There's a video message on the file, but I can't share it with you.'

'Please can you make an exception for me?' I said. I knew I was coming across as desperate and was probably making things worse. 'I can't sleep because I'm so worried. Please, play the video. Just this once.'

The woman shrugged. 'Even if you convinced me, the system wouldn't let me. You'd need to return with the person who paid for the treatment. They'd have to give me their permission and I'd have to enter their card details.'

She stood up and waited at the door.

'All I can tell you is that there's usually a very good reason people are brought here for treatment,' she said. 'Trust me. You'd be better off leaving it.'

'I suppose you're right,' I said.

I plodded back down the long path away from the clinic. I passed a man with his arm around a sobbing woman, maybe his wife.

I wondered what she needed to forget about. But this just made me even more desperate to find out who had taken me here, what had been wiped from my mind and what it had to do with Adam.

CHAPTER 4
THE VIDEO

By the time I was home, I'd worked it all out. I thought about the night I'd tried to come out to my parents. Dad had ignored me and he'd never mentioned it since.

I'd assumed he'd felt awkward because I'd talked about personal stuff, but what if there was more to it than that? What if he actually disapproved? What if he was so angry about it he'd taken me to The Loftus Clinic to have all my memories of my only ever boyfriend removed?

I must have agreed to it, because I wrote down the date and reference number. But maybe I

didn't know what I was agreeing to. Maybe
I thought I was going for a dental check-up
or something.

I threw the living room door wide open when
I got home. Instead of just muting the TV, I
grabbed the remote and turned it off.

'Does The Loftus Clinic mean anything to you?'
I asked.

'We were watching that,' said Mum. This wasn't
even true, she was looking at her phone when I
came in.

Dad leapt up and tried to grab the remote. I
pulled it back, out of his reach.

'Did you think you could change me just by
taking away my memories of my boyfriend?'
I asked.

'I don't know what you're talking about,' said
Dad. He snatched the remote and put his show
back on.

'Are you feeling alright?' asked Mum. She'd put her phone down and was staring at me.

They seemed genuinely confused. The name of The Loftus Clinic hadn't rung a bell, but I had no idea how the treatment worked. Maybe they'd wiped their own memories too.

I had to calm down and work out what to do. I went up to bed and pulled the covers over my head.

The woman with red hair had said that whoever had paid for the treatment would need to go back with their card details. But I'd never be able to convince Dad to do that if he didn't even remember taking me in the first place.

There was a way around it. I could take Dad's card from his wallet while he was asleep, go back to the clinic and pretend it was mine. They'd put the details into their computer and I could watch the video.

No doubt it would show Dad telling me he was doing it for my own good and that one day I'd understand or some such rubbish.

But at least then I'd know for sure that he'd taken me to the clinic. After that, who knows? Maybe I'd sit down and calmly discuss it with him. Or maybe I'd take his precious TV and throw it out of the window.

I set my alarm for six. I knew Dad didn't wake up until seven, which would give me plenty of time to grab his card.

It seemed like the volume had been turned up on the house as I crept downstairs. I'm sure the floorboards had never creaked that loudly before.

Dad's jacket was draped over the side of the sofa. I felt awful about taking his debit card, but I had to remind myself why I was doing it. If I was right, he'd stolen something much more important than bank details from me.

I pulled the door shut. There were no noises of stirring from upstairs.

The streets were virtually empty as I made my way to the industrial estate. The clinic surely wouldn't be open until at least nine, but I didn't mind waiting. All I could think about was getting back in and finding out the truth. I'd worry about giving Dad his card back and getting to school later.

I arrived at The Loftus Clinic just after seven. I expected to have to stand outside the fence for a couple of hours, but the security guard ushered me in as soon as I reeled off my reference number. I wondered if the place ran all night like a hospital emergency ward.

Inside, I gave my reference number to the receptionist and I was shown into another of the small meeting rooms.

This time I was seen by a woman with curly black hair who was sipping coffee from a cup with The

Loftus Clinic's logo on it. I was glad it wasn't the woman with red hair. I could hardly pretend to be casually checking my account if she remembered me begging her to tell me about it in our last meeting.

'How can I help you?' she asked.

'I need to check the video message on a memory wipe program I paid for,' I said. 'Here's the card I used.'

I lifted Dad's debit card out of my pocket. I was worried she'd notice my hand was trembling, so I threw the card onto the desk instead of handing it over.

The woman tapped the number into her computer. She pressed enter and took another swig of coffee.

'Sorry,' she said, 'our system isn't recognising this card. Are you sure it's the one you used?'

I took my wallet out again and pretended to search for an alternative. I hadn't thought about what I'd do if the card didn't work.

It looked as though the whole trip had been a waste of time. At least they'd seen me early enough for me to go home, sneak Dad's card back into his wallet and make it to school on time.

A possibility occurred to me. It didn't make any sense, but I thought I might as well check it out.

I handed over my own debit card.

The woman typed the details in.

'Yep, this is the right one,' she said. She leaned back in her chair and sipped her coffee. 'Here's your video.'

She angled her screen around and clicked play.

The video showed another white room with a white desk. And sitting behind the desk, talking into the camera, was me.

CHAPTER 5
THE TRUTH

'Are you sure you want to watch this?' asked the woman. 'We can't take any responsibility if it distresses you.'

'It's fine,' I said. 'Keep it going.'

I watched myself speaking. I sounded pretty calm at first, but my voice soon cracked and tears began to run down my cheeks:

'I, Ryan Watson, give full consent for The Loftus Clinic to remove all memories of my ex-boyfriend Adam Mason. I will not hold the clinic to account for any side effects.

'This is my statement for the records of The Loftus Clinic.

'Adam dumped me last week. Things have been really rough since then. But two days ago I made a decision. I wasn't going to put myself through it any more. I'd heard rumours about this clinic and eventually I managed to arrange a meeting and they agreed to treat me.

'In just under an hour, I'll have no memory of ever having had a boyfriend. It will be as though I had never met Adam, and that's exactly what I want.'

It's always weird watching yourself on film. You never quite look or sound like you think you're going to. But this was off the scale. I felt like reaching into the screen and giving myself a hug.

The woman in the white coat kept sipping coffee and glancing between me and the screen. Watching someone delivering a secret message to themselves didn't seem to bother her at all.

I guessed it was just a normal day at the office for her.

'Did you find out everything you wanted?' she asked.

'Yeah,' I said. 'Thanks.'

She gave the bank cards back to me and I slid them into my wallet.

'How would you rate your experience with The Loftus Clinic today on a scale of one to five, with one being very unsatisfied and five being very satisfied?' she asked.

'What?' I asked. My head was still spinning. 'I don't know. It was just really weird.'

'I'll put you down as a five,' said the woman, clicking her mouse.

I walked home from the industrial estate in a daze. At least now I knew who to be angry with – myself.

I know I had been upset about Adam finishing with me. But wiping him from my memory was stupid. Coping with the break-up would have been hard, but piecing everything back together had been even tougher.

Mum and Dad were having a massive row when I got home. Dad couldn't leave for work without his bank card and Mum was telling him to be more careful with his stuff.

I tossed his card next to the vase on the hallway table and shouted through the door that I was too sick for school.

As I lay on my bed, I heard Mum discover the card, but it didn't stop the argument. I could hear her telling Dad it proved her point about him being careless.

I felt guilty about taking Dad's card and assuming everything was his fault. But admitting the truth now would only make things worse.

Besides, there was someone I felt even guiltier about.

I picked up my phone and sent Adam a message:

Sorry about everything that happened. Call and I'll explain.

I sat on my bed staring at my phone and waiting for a reply. It didn't come. I told myself that Adam was probably at school and that I should be patient. I could only hold out for twenty minutes before sending another message:

I was wrong when I said I didn't remember you. I know you were telling the truth now, but it's complicated.

There was still no reply an hour later, so I tried again:

Adam, we need to talk.

I still hadn't heard from him by half five. Surely he was out of lessons now.

It must have been confusing for him. I had spent ages telling him to stop calling and now I was desperate to get in touch.

At six I tried ringing him. I tried again a few minutes later. A few minutes after that he finally sent me a message:

I have no idea who you are. Don't contact me again.

CHAPTER 6
THE STRANGER

After 100 false starts, I'd finally found him.

It was Saturday afternoon and I'd been waiting on the corner of Station Road and North Road since early in the morning.

Adam had refused to take my calls all week. I'd come back to the place where he'd approached me because it was all I had to go on. I didn't know where he lived, or where he went to school, or anything about him at all except that we used to be a couple.

Now he was actually here. I waved and strode towards him.

'Adam, it's me,' I said.

He took a step backwards and yanked one of his headphones from his ear.

'I think you were right,' I said. 'We should get back together.'

Adam shrugged. 'I'm sorry,' he said, 'I think you've got the wrong guy.'

'I get it,' I said. 'This is what I did to you. Now you're doing the same. I understand, but we really need to talk.'

Adam put his earbud back in and tried to push past.

'I've been to The Loftus Clinic,' I said. 'I found out what happened.'

'Never heard of it,' he said. 'And I've no idea who you are.'

He stepped around me, pressed the remote on his headphones and continued down Station Road.

'You sent me hundreds of texts!' I shouted. 'You called me over and over again. So why are you ignoring me now?'

He kept going. A woman with a pram and a man in a leather jacket were staring at me, but Adam didn't look back.

I wondered why he said he hadn't heard of the Loftus Clinic. I was sure he'd told me otherwise.

I looked back through our texts and found:

Ever heard of The Loftus Clinic?

He replied with:

Yeah, you mentioned it.

And then with:

Fine. You win.

Now I understood what he meant. He thought I was telling him to go to the clinic himself and get his memories of me wiped, which is what he'd done.

So he was telling the truth when he said he had no idea who I was.

Two weeks ago, I'd thought he was a mad stalker who believed he knew me. Now the tables had turned and I was the crazy one.

Adam was down at the far end of the street now. I watched him until he was out of sight.

ABOUT THE AUTHOR

Tim Collins is originally from Manchester, but now lives near London. He has written more than 60 books, including *Wimpy Superhero*, *Dorkius Maximus*, *Cosmic Colin*, *Monstrous Maud* and *The League of Enchanted Heroes*. He has won awards in the UK and Germany.